Impressum:
Hanna Roth
c/o COCENTER
Koppoldstr. 1
86551 Aichach

Hannas
ROTH

@hannaroths Halloween-ABC-Coloring-Book

Check also out:

"Nerdy-Halloween-Greetings"

"Kreatives Blumen-ABC-Malbuch"

"Kreatives-Fantasie-
Tier-ABC-Malbuch"

"Animal-ABC-Coloring-Book"

"Dating Proverbs:
Ancient Wisdom for Modern Love"

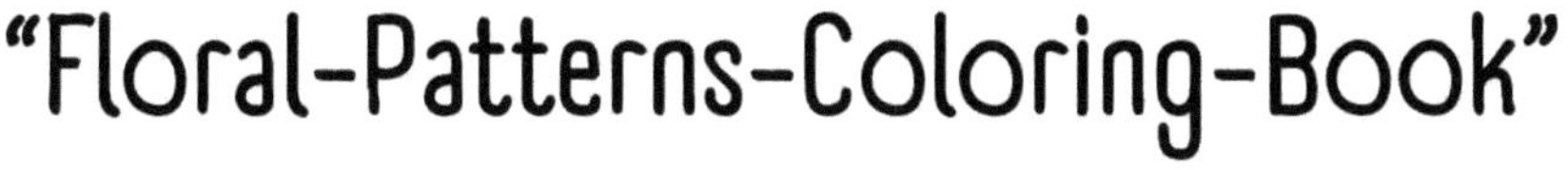
"Floral-Patterns-Coloring-Book"